PLANTING A GARDEN IN ROOM 6

WRITTEN AND PHOTOGRAPHED BY
CAROLINE ARNOLD

PLANTING A GARDEN IN ROOM 6

FROM SEEDS TO SALAD

Charlesbridge

THE CHILDREN IN ROOM 6 ARE PLANTING A VEGETABLE GARDEN.

Their teacher, Mrs. Best, has brought seeds and young plants to school. The children will plant them in a sunny spot outside their classroom in large wooden boxes filled with soil. Soon lettuce, radishes, spinach, peas, and other vegetables will begin to grow. How long until they are ready to pick?

spinach
seeds

beet seeds

pea seeds

lettuce
seeds

radish
seeds

Every plant has its own kind of seeds.
Each seed has everything it needs to
make a new plant.

Mrs. Best has chosen plants that grow well in the cool weather of early spring. Most of the vegetables will be ready to harvest before the end of the school year.

Plants cannot grow when the ground is frozen. But some plants, like lettuce and peas, can survive a light frost.

green onions

cauliflower

broccoli

kale

Before the children can begin planting, they must prepare the soil. They pull out old plants and weeds. They mix in dead leaves and grass clippings, which will add nutrients to the soil.

They also add earthworms to the garden. The worms wiggle into the ground. Their tunnels keep the soil loose so air and water can get in.

Worms help keep garden soil healthy. They eat old leaves and dead plants. Their body waste fertilizes the soil.

Plants can grow in any kind of container as long as the soil is deep enough for the plant roots. Soil contains minerals that plants need to grow.

The garden rows are twelve inches apart. This will give the plants room to spread out as they grow.

Each packet of seeds has instructions for planting. They tell how deep to plant each seed and how far apart the seeds should be.

The children take turns planting the seeds in rows. Mrs. Best has put strings across each garden box to help keep the rows straight.

Along each row the children poke a line of holes. They drop in seeds one by one and cover them with soil.

The kale, green onion, broccoli, and cauliflower plants were started from seeds in a nursery. It is time to transplant them from their tiny pots to the garden bed.

The children dig a hole for each plant. They carefully place the roots in the hole and cover them with soil.

It takes a week or so for transplanted seedlings to get used to their new home. Then they will start growing new leaves.

All plants need water. Unless it rains, the children water the garden every day.

Under the moist soil the seeds begin to grow. In about a week the first green shoots will poke up into the sunshine.

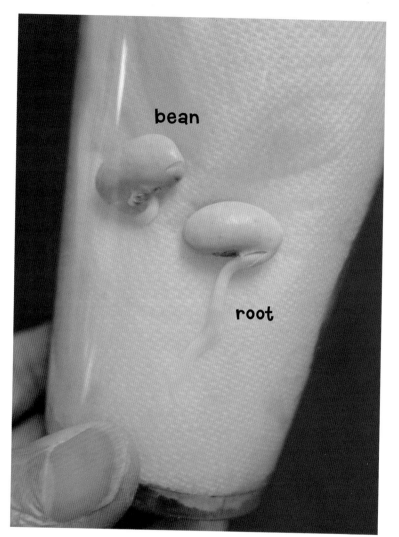

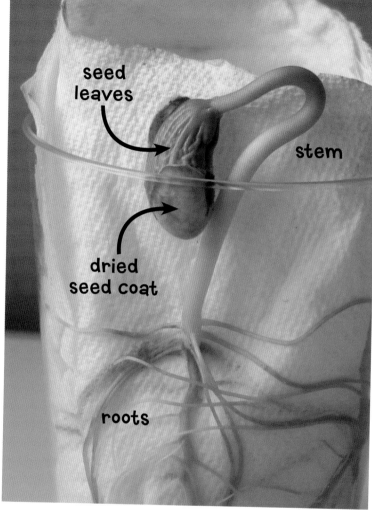

Each bean is covered by a thin layer called a seed coat. As the moist seed swells, the seed coat splits and a root begins to grow. Roots take in water for the plant.

A few days later more roots and a stem begin to grow. The seed coat dries up and falls off. Underneath are the seed leaves. They contain the plant's first food.

true leaves

seed leaves

The stem grows taller, and the seed leaves split. Tiny green leaves peek out. These true leaves will use sunlight to make food for the plant.

While the children wait, they learn how seeds grow. Inside each seed is the beginning of a new plant, called an embryo.

Dried beans are seeds. The children put beans in plastic cups lined with wet paper towels. The water soaks the beans, and they begin to grow. Over the next two weeks, the beans develop roots, stems, and finally the first leaves.

true leaves

seed leaves

In two weeks the bean plants have grown tall. The seed leaves have shrunk as their food is used up.

pea seedlings

THE SEEDS IN THE GARDEN ARE GROWING, TOO!

Tiny green leaves push up through the soil. The peas are the first to come up. After a week they are one inch tall. The carrots, spinach, lettuce, beets, and radishes are sprouting, too.

carrot seedlings

spinach seedlings

The children are excited to see all the seedlings. But some of the plants are too crowded. It is time to thin them out.

Carefully the children pull out some of the tiny seedlings. They leave the largest plants in the soil. Now the plants will have plenty of room for their leaves to spread out and for their roots to grow underground.

lettuce seedlings

beet seedlings

A seedling is a very young plant. Each kind of plant has its own kind of leaves.

radish seedlings

Mrs. Best gives some of the thinned seedlings to the school chickens as a special treat.

The rest of the thinned seedlings go into a compost bin. Compost is decayed plant material that can be used as plant fertilizer.

In a compost bin, plant waste slowly rots and releases nutrients. When the compost is ready, it can be added to garden soil.

compost bin

The school chickens live in a pen next to the play yard. Every day the children feed them and collect their eggs. In addition to grain, chickens eat small plants, seeds, and insects.

Day by day the plants in the garden grow bigger.

In a month the pea plants are so tall they are falling over. Mrs. Best puts up a trellis so they have something to hang on to as they climb.

Most vegetable plants need at least six hours of sunshine a day.

Some plants grow fast. Others grow more slowly. After seven weeks the first radishes are big enough to pick. The children pull them out of the ground and wash them. Everyone gets a crunchy taste.

broccoli

The plants in the garden keep growing.

At eight weeks the broccoli leaves are as big as the children's hands.

After ten weeks the cauliflower plants have tiny buds.

At twelve weeks the pea plants produce their first flowers. Soon the flowers will develop into pea pods.

cauliflower

pea flowers

aphids

ladybugs

One day the children discover tiny aphids eating the broccoli and cauliflower plants. Aphids are insects that kill plants by sucking the juices from the stems and leaves.

Ladybugs are a natural predator of aphids. Mrs. Best brings some ladybugs to school and lets them go in the garden. They will eat the aphids and keep them from harming the plants.

Many insects help a garden grow. Bees and butterflies carry pollen from flower to flower. Pill bugs enrich the soil with their body waste.

peas

Three months have gone by. The plants have grown bigger and bigger. The vegetables are ready to pick.

broccoli

IT'S HARVEST TIME!

Mrs. Best and the children pick peas, carrots, lettuce, radishes, spinach, beets, green onions, kale, broccoli, and cauliflower. They wash the vegetables and make a salad.

Some vegetables taste good eaten raw. Others need to be cooked.

FROM SEEDS TO SALAD!

Nothing tastes as good as vegetables fresh from the garden. Especially when you have grown them yourself.

WHaT PaRTS OF PLaNTS DO We eaT?

Stems: We eat the stems of plants like celery and asparagus.

Leaves: Lettuce, spinach, kale, and parsley are some of the many leaf vegetables. Beet leaves can also be eaten.

Roots: Radishes, carrots, and beets are all roots that we eat.

Seeds: Peas and beans are seeds that grow inside pods. Rice, corn, and wheat are also seeds. They can be ground into flour.

Bulbs: Onions and leeks are bulbs. A bulb is an underground bud enclosed in thick, over-lapping leaves.

Flowers: Cauliflower and broccoli are flower buds. We eat them before the flowers bloom.

Tubers: Potatoes and yams are tubers. Tubers form underground at the base of the plant roots.

Fruits: Tomatoes and pumpkins are fruits. A fruit contains the seeds of a flowering plant. We eat the fleshy part around the seeds.

GARDEN TOOLS

garden **fork** for loosening soil

spade for digging big holes

hoe for digging up plants

trowel for digging small holes

cultivator for breaking up soil

watering can

GARDEN QUESTIONS

What can I plant in my garden?

Every garden is different. What you plant will depend on the time of year, the climate where you live, and the location of your garden. A local garden store can help you choose the best seeds and plants for your area. Mrs. Best and her students live in Southern California. Their growing season for cool-weather vegetables begins in late winter.

Do I need to start with seeds?

No. Many vegetable plants take several months to grow from seed to harvest. You can shorten your gardening time by starting with young plants.

What makes plants green?

Plants have a substance called chlorophyll that makes them green. They use chlorophyll to trap sunlight.

How do plants make their own food?

They use the energy in sunlight to turn water and carbon dioxide into sugar. This process is called photosynthesis.

Which kinds of beans can you sprout in a cup?

You can use any dried bean usually used for cooking, such as pinto or lima beans. The children in Room 6 used Great Northern beans. To grow beans in your garden, it is best to get seeds from a garden store.

How long does it take for vegetables to grow?

It depends on the vegetable and the growing conditions. Radishes and lettuce can be ready to pick after six weeks. Carrots and peas take longer. The back of the seed packet tells how long the seeds take to reach maturity.

We pick and eat some vegetables, like lettuce and beets, before they produce seeds. But if they are left in the garden to complete their growth cycle, they will develop flowers and seeds.

GARDEN VOCABULARY

aphid: a tiny insect that sucks plant sap.

chlorophyll: a green substance that plants use to trap sunlight for photosynthesis.

compost: a mix of dead plants, decaying leaves, vegetable scraps, and other plant material. Microorganisms (tiny living things), worms, and insects break down this mixture and turn it into nutrients for the soil.

embryo: the beginning of a new plant in a seed.

fertilizer: a substance added to the soil as food for plants.

fruit: the part of a flowering plant that contains the seeds.

leaves: plant parts that use sunlight to make the sugar the plant needs to grow.

mineral: a chemical substance formed naturally in the earth, such as calcium, iron, or sodium.

nursery: a place that grows and sells young plants.

nutrients: substances that living things need to build and fuel their bodies.

photosynthesis: the process of using sunlight to turn water and carbon dioxide into the sugar a plant needs to grow.

pollen: a fine powder, usually yellow, that is produced by flowers and used to make seeds.

roots: the parts of a plant that hold it in place as it grows. Roots take in water and minerals from the soil.

seed: the part of a seed-producing plant that can grow into a new plant. Each seed contains a plant embryo and the food the embryo needs to grow.

seed coat: the covering of a seed.

seed leaves: a plant's first leaves. Seed leaves contain food the plant uses until it grows true leaves.

seedling: a young plant that has grown from a seed.

soil: a mixture of minerals, water, air, living matter, and the decaying remains of once-living things.

stems: the parts of a plant that support its leaves. Stems carry water and minerals from the roots to the leaves.

transplant: to move a plant to a new location where it can continue growing.

trellis: a framework that supports climbing plants.

weeds: unwanted plants that compete for water, space, and sunlight with the plants a gardener wants to grow.

ONLINE SOURCES

Growing Calendar

https://gilmour.com/planting-calendar
When to plant vegetables outdoors in your location (planting zones).

Your Go-To Guide for Gardening with Children

https://gardenerspath.com/how-to/beginners/gardening-children/
Helpful advice for gardening with children, from supply lists and planting guides to activities and soil science.

Plants for Pre-K Gardens

https://kidsgardening.org/gardening-basics-plants-for-pre-k-gardens/
Includes recommendations for cool-season and warm-season plants.

Composting

https://kidsgardening.org/gardening-basics-composting/
Definition and benefits of composting, and how to make compost.

The URLs listed here were accurate at publication, but websites often change. If a URL doesn't work, you can use the internet to find more information.

FURTHER READING

From Seed to Plant by Gail Gibbons (Holiday House, 1991)
How seeds grow into plants. Includes a project for raising bean plants.

Gardening with Children by Monika Hannemann, Patricia Hulse, Brian Johnson, Barbara Kurland, and Tracey Patterson (Brooklyn Botanic Garden, Inc., 2007)
Fact-filled activity guide for adults to use when gardening with children.

Plants Feed Me by Lizzie Rockwell (Holiday House, 2014)
The different parts of plants we use for food.

Rah, Rah, Radishes! A Vegetable Chant by April Pulley Sayre (Beach Lane Books, 2011)
Read-aloud chant celebrating vegetables found in farmers' markets.

The Vegetables We Eat by Gail Gibbons (Holiday House, 2007)
The different categories of vegetables and how they are grown.

One Little Lot: The 1-2-3s of an Urban Garden by Diane C. Mullen (Charlesbridge, 2020)
Fictional story about a neighborhood that turns an abandoned lot into a community vegetable garden.

ACKNOWLEDGMENTS

I thank Jennifer Best and her kindergarten students at Haynes Charter for Enriched Studies, Los Angeles, California, for sharing their garden activities with me. I am grateful to the children's parents and the school principal, Barbara Meade, for their enthusiastic support. Most of all, I appreciate Jennifer's cheerful cooperation on this project. I couldn't have done this book without her. This is our third book together. The chicken pictured on page 21 hatched four years ago when Jennifer and I worked together on *Hatching Chicks in Room 6*. Two of the grown chicks now live in an enclosure at the school.

To Jennifer Best, her students,
and their families

First paperback edition 2024
Copyright © 2022 by Caroline Arnold
All rights reserved, including the right of reproduction in whole or
    in part in any form. Charlesbridge and colophon are registered
    trademarks of Charlesbridge Publishing, Inc.

At the time of publication, any URLs printed in this book were accurate
and active. Charlesbridge and the author are not responsible for the
content or accessibility of any website.

Published by Charlesbridge
9 Galen Street
Watertown, MA 02472
(617) 926-0329
www.charlesbridge.com

Library of Congress Cataloging-in-Publication Data
Names: Arnold, Caroline, author.
Title: Planting a garden in room 6: from seeds to salad / Caroline Arnold.
Description: Watertown, MA: Charlesbridge, [2022] | Audience: Ages 3-7 |
    Audience: Grades K-1 | Summary: "Follow a classroom of diverse
    kindergartners as they plant seeds in their garden, tend the growing
    plants, and harvest the vegetables. Clear, bright photographs show the
    plant life cycle."–Provided by publisher.
Identifiers: LCCN 2020052059 (print) | LCCN 2020052060 (ebook) |
    ISBN 9781623542405 (hardcover) | ISBN 9781623544300 (paperback) |
    ISBN 9781632896728 (ebook)
Subjects: LCSH: Plant life cycles–Juvenile literature. | Growth (Plants)–
    Juvenile literature.
Classification: LCC QK731 .A755 2022 (print) | LCC QK731 (ebook) |
    DDC 571.8/2–dc23
LC record available at https://lccn.loc.gov/2020052059
LC ebook record available at https://lccn.loc.gov/2020052060

Printed in China
(hc) 10 9 8 7 6 5 4 3 2 1
(pb) 10 9 8 7 6 5 4 3 2 1

Display type set in Swung Note by PintassilgoPrints, Family Dog Fat
    by Pizzadude.dk, and Poplar by Barbara Lind
Text type set in Jesterday by Jelloween Foundry
Printed by 1010 Printing International Limited in Huizhou, Guangdong, China
Production supervision by Jennifer Most Delaney
Designed by Cathleen Schaad